LEADING
with

and
A Journey of Organizational
Culture Change

Melissa,
May you always
lead with
grit & grace.
Ashleigh

ASHLEIGH WALTERS

Printed in the United States of America

First Printing, 2020

ISBN 978-0-578-79597-3

Library of Congress Control Number: 2020917734

Cover and book design, Susan Malikowski

Editing, PJ Dempsey

Copyediting, Greta Langhenry

Proofreading, Gage Cogswell

Printed in the U.S.A.

ashleigh.walters@onexinc.com

onexinc.com/make-things-better/leading-with-grit-and-grace

To my husband: Drew, my counterpart
in love and life always encouraging me
to step outside my comfort zone.

And, to my boys: Jackson and Carson,
your creativity inspires me to
think outside the box.

Contents

Introduction vii

1 The Road Less Traveled 11

2 Change is Necessary 21

3 Freedom to Fail 33

4 Servant Leadership 43

5 A Coach Approach 55

6 Mission Critical 69

7 Sales and Marketing 81

8 Crisis Management 93

9   Leave it Better 105

10 Amazing Grace 117

    References 121

    Acknowledgments 123

    About the Author 127

    Lessons to Lead By 129

Introduction

In March of 2017, I was honored to address the entire Pennsylvania delegation of United States congressmen and senators. I was excited to share my story, and even though I knew a lot about the importance of manufacturing as it relates to the American economy, I was still nervous. The night before I left for Washington, D.C., my younger son asked me if I really had to go. I asked him if he knew what manufacturing meant, and he rolled his eyes and replied, "Yes, it means we make stuff!"

That is true, because as manufacturers, we turn ideas into real things. We make street signposts out of recycled railroad ties and airplane parts out of molten aluminum. These real things have real value that creates jobs and economic stability for industry employees, their families, and our communities.

I am a small-town girl from a multi-generational manufacturing family. I was raised in a tradition steeped in determination, resilience and persistence. I call this "GRIT." So, when it came time to choose an engineering college, Auburn University seemed like a natural fit for me. Not only is Auburn located in a small town, but also its creed begins "I can only count on what I earn. Therefore, I believe in work, hard work," and, after all the hard work it took to earn my engineering degree, I learned to lead with empathy and compassion for others. I call this "GRACE."

So, in the spirit of Grit and Grace, I promised myself that unless I had a very good reason not to, I would always say "yes" when asked to tell my story, and I have remained true to my word. I have been asked to speak at the national summit for Women in Manufacturing, in front of the Commonwealth of Pennsylvania's legislature's Manufacturing Caucus, and at

Penn State Behrend's engineering department, just to name a few. Each time someone thanks me (sometimes with tears in their eyes) for sharing my story, it fills me with pride, because I know that I have made an impact on his or her life. It also validates the decisions I have made and reminds me that the lessons I learned have universal appeal and can benefit others.

That is why I wrote this book. It is meant to be a small gift to you. Sharing the knowledge I have gained over the years rescuing and running a company is my way of paying it forward. It is my wish that you are inspired by the changes I made at Onex and draw from what I did to strategize your own plan. It doesn't matter what type of company you are leading, because inspiring personnel, making hard decisions, and celebrating success are what get us to the ultimate goal of leaving things better than we found them.

So here I am, working in a gritty industry and leading with grace while still wearing my pearls (at least some days) as homage to my Southern roots. It is not lost on me that a pearl exists as the result of an irritating piece of grit that made its way into an oyster. It takes years for the grit to transform into a pearl. To me, this symbolizes that wisdom is gained through experiences, some of which are not always comfortable, but that if you act with gratitude as your guiding light, something beautiful can be created.

Let's make things better together!

Chapter One

The Road Less Traveled

Two roads diverged in a wood, and I—
I took the one less traveled by,
And that has made all the difference.
~ Robert Frost

In October of 2013, my father-in-law called to let me know that the CFO of his company had left. He asked me to lead Onex, a family-owned, 50-year-old, industrial furnace service business. It's hard enough to take charge of a business that is doing well, but this one was, to say the least, in disarray. The employees were not working together as a team and were actually pitted against one another, while others had a "not my job" attitude. All the business units were siloed. The previous CFO led through fear. We were no longer the friendly "family" company we once had been where people loved to come to work. So, there I was, trying to build trust in a team who had been betrayed by their former boss and did not know me, and with a business that was in severe financial distress, but I was motivated and determined to figure out a way to turn the business around.

My road to business success was truly the road less traveled. You see—my education was in engineering, not in business management. Even though I had no idea what strategies the business books would have suggested for solving my dilemma of trying to turn around a distressed business, my background came through in spades, because engineering taught me to solve a problem by knowing how to find a solution. When I began my career, my father was quick to tell me that just because I had a degree in engineering that did not mean I knew more than the personnel on the plant floor. He stressed that in order to put my degree to work and make the textbook learning practical, I had to ask the people on the frontlines doing the actual work their perspectives. These individuals very likely knew the solution to the problem I was working on but had never before been asked by management for their input. So, I set out to explore on the road less traveled by identifying problems and creating solutions.

That advice from my father proved invaluable as I began asking these troubled employees questions about the processes. At first, they were skeptical, which was understandable based on their former manager's style. They feared I was fishing for what they had done wrong and would berate them. I had to convince them that this was the previous CFO's management style—not mine. I truly wanted to know how we were doing things so I could understand the jobs and the business well enough to suggest ways we could make improvements. I started by hanging up "think outside the box" signs on the walls in every plant and office. I requested suggestions on how we could make things better. When a suggestion resulted in a process improvement or cost savings, I gave the employee a think outside the box trophy and a handwritten letter of gratitude—everything was positive. My authenticity, transparency and humility slowly allowed me to earn the trust of my employees. The more we improved the business by working together, the better everyone felt. We celebrated our successes together as a team and planned the problem we would tackle next.

What I learned was that when everyone knows their voice is being heard and their suggestions are considered meaningful, they speak more freely and have pride in and loyalty to their jobs. Employers might pay an employee for his or her hands, but when these employees feel psychologically safe, they give their hearts and heads as well.

My message to all business leaders is that everyone in an organization needs and wants to know that their work is important for the greater good, so you should start with an attainable mission that everyone can get behind and play a part in achieving. This mission will drive every decision that you make as an organization. In other words, this mission will be your guiding light.

Know Your Why And What

Your "Why" is what gives you the passion and energy to pursue the challenges ahead, no matter how dire they may seem in the moment.

Several years ago, a vendor visited Onex to compare the two companies' synergies and see how we could further work together. We had a PowerPoint presentation of all our product lines and a plant tour prepared—isn't that what you are supposed to do? After our presentation, the vendor asked one simple question that changed our course as a company.

What do you want the company to be when it grows up?

Onex had spent years saying "yes" any time a client asked if we could do something. We had grown opportunistically, but not strategically. There was no mission by which to guide our decisions. The goal was essentially, "Be everything to everyone." Unfortunately, when you try to do everything, you don't do any one thing as well as you could. And, when you are in the midst of an economic downturn, you may find yourself with too many resources devoted to failing product lines and not enough income.

Constructing a Mission Statement

Because the mission statement is the guide for all of the company's actions, it's important to get right. The following is the process I used to find Onex's mission statement:

My first stab at it was:

"Onex is committed to providing unique, cost-effective solutions for our customers. We aim to deliver exceptional value by producing high-quality products, optimizing processes, and eliminating waste in the total value stream."

That doesn't exactly fill you up with energy and make you want to be a part of the team, now does it? This first try was just like most generic mission statements, in that it contained lots of words that were pretty uninspiring and stated the things a company is supposed to be doing anyway. What I needed was to have a heart-to-heart conversation with my employees about what inspired them to get out of bed each morning. In this instance, I found Simon Sinek's book, *Start with Why: How Great Leaders Inspire Everyone to Take Action*, to be an incredible help. In it, Sinek explains something called the "Golden Circle" and how most companies communicate. Everyone will tell you what he or she does, some of them will tell you how they do it, but very few will tell you *why* they do what they do. This is important, because customer loyalty is not built on features and benefits, but on shared beliefs and values.

A Mission Increases Success

Knowing your mission increases your chances of success. Here are four reasons why:

Direction: Your mission statement should be the driving force behind everything you and your employees do. It is the reminder of why you exist and what you are selling.

Decisions: Following a predetermined set of boundaries can help you quickly and confidently make good decisions.

Strategy: Your business strategy should not follow that of your competitors'. Their plan may work for them, but not for you. Use your mission to help form a healthy approach to achieving what you set out to do.

Improvement: If you are not doing your best, you are probably not serving your mission. Your mission should be your standard—always work to achieve it and more.

Every company wants its team to wake up excited to come to work, feel safe both physically and emotionally, and return home fulfilled by their job. Every employee wants to know that their work is important for the greater good of society. So, your organization must have a mission that everyone can get behind. Never forget that your mission is what drives your every decision, and the reason for following it, your "Why," gives you and your team the passion and energy to pursue the challenges ahead.

My new and revised mission statement for Onex evolved into:

Make Things Better: empowered employees, happy customers and thriving communities.

People want to know how they can help make the world a better place. This revision was important, because creating jobs is exciting. There's an employment multiplier effect, which means our mission ultimately improves society by creating jobs and strengthening a community's economy. For instance, American Certified reports that for every manufacturing job created, there are an additional 4.6 new support jobs created in the community, such as grocery store clerks, teachers, and restaurant staff. Doesn't all that job creation feel amazing?

—— REFLECTION ——

Take some time to review your personal or company mission statement. Make sure it instills in you the energy required to forge the road ahead while navigating the potholes in order to reach your destination. If it doesn't, it's time to rethink your mission.

Chapter Two

Change Is Necessary

There are no big problems,
there are just a lot of little problems.
~ Henry Ford

In 1910, the Ford Motor Company was one of many small automobile manufacturers. A decade later, Ford had obtained a 60 percent market share of the new automobile market worldwide. According to its website, Ford reduced assembly time per vehicle from 12 and a half hours to 90 minutes, and the price from $850 to $300, while also paying employees competitive rates.

Henry Ford and Frederick Taylor, a theorist and

the "father of scientific management," used the scientific method to optimize labor productivity, which resulted in the streamlining of the assembly line and mass-production of cars, which in turn ushered in a new era of unprecedented efficiency. For decades, the organizations that embraced this mass production or "machine model," dominated their markets, outperformed their competitors, and drew the best talent. The one-hundred-year period from 1911 to 2011 became what we now refer to as "the management century." Command-and-control, top-down management was the preferred style.

But, as Henry Ford said, "There are no big problems, there are just a lot of little problems." This encapsulates how I feel about organizational culture today—not much has changed. "It has always been this way" is a statement I hear a lot, but just because it has always been doesn't mean it is what is right for today's ever-changing business environment. There is a paradigm shift underway, and often, even changes that are needed tend to be disruptive.

We are no strangers to disruption these days.

Uber, Airbnb, and Netflix are just a few companies that quickly come to mind that have disrupted the way traditional businesses operate in today's world. If you are a taxi company, you are likely feeling a little salty about the new kid on the block, Uber. The same goes for the traditional TV networks being disrupted by on-demand content like Netflix. Personally, I love staying in an Airbnb over a hotel because it feels more like home—I don't have to eat out if I don't want to and I can wash my clothes before I head back home. If the traditional players, who once dominated their fields, would have been more aware of or done a better job at meeting their customers' ever-changing needs, these new companies with their innovative management techniques and creative ways of doing business may have never been invented at all.

I believe traditional organizations need to combat their new and disruptive competitors by becoming more agile through promoting an empowered workplace culture. Yes, I know old business tactics die hard and the people who run them are set in their old ways, but it is possible to maintain a stable backbone on which to support the core business while creating the dynamic capabilities necessary for adapting quickly to new challenges and opportunities.

We need to simply think of this shift as a renovation project. Organizations with strong bones should need to update only their interiors, for example, rethinking how the business can utilize technology to become more efficient and agile, just like Ford utilized scientific systems in his era, and by returning power to personnel and not impeding them with nonsense restrictions but instead empowering them to make changes to their work processes responsibly, thereby increasing their efficiency.

The Mindset Shift

Will this change to the way business has been done traditionally be easy? No. Will it happen quickly? Again, no. Most days it will feel like you are running a 50-year-old startup. To counter this feeling, you need to solve three little problems, which will result in a mindset shift, allowing for a transformational change to take place and an agile, empowered workplace culture to be created.

Shared Mission: Make sure your company's mission allows stakeholders to feel personally and emotionally invested. (Notice I said *stake*holders and not *share*holders.) Stakeholders are shareholders, but more importantly, this group includes personnel, clients, vendors, and the community. Agile organizations are intensely customer focused, allowing for unprecedented variety and customization across the entire customer life cycle. These organizations are poised to listen to their customers and create value based on their clients' unique needs.

Employee Engagement: Get rid of that tired, old hierarchical bureaucratic chart that is a holdover from Ford's management century. Create clear, flat structures clustered into focused performance groups. Ensure that each team member has a clear role and is accountable so he or she can interact across the organization and get work done with limited required manager approval. Create active partnerships with external networks to access the best talent and available ideas. Design an open environment that fosters transparency, communication, and collaboration. No silos or internal competition allowed.

Rapid Cycles of Thinking and Doing: Focus on rapidly changing and adapting as new technology emerges. To be agile, you need to create continuous iterations of identifying, experimenting, and learning to foster an innovative environment. Rather than yearly planning cycles, try shorter-term cycles—perhaps quarterly—for meeting goals and metrics. Technology is changing quickly. Can we ever really know what the next five to ten years will look like?

The Lean Journey

You already know how important it is to have a shared mission with your employees. Now, let's talk about the benefit of having engaged employees along on your journey to success. These subjects go hand in hand, as I found out. Together, they shaped the journey I took to train empowered, engaged employees.

What does the word "Lean" mean in this context?

Toyota developed "Lean" in the middle of the 20th century to increase manufacturing efficiency in its production operations. Toyota needed to compete in automobile production against the Big Three United States auto manufacturers. However, Toyota did not have the resources that the Big Three did, so it had to reduce waste and non-value-added steps in its processes.

Our Lean journey began when we mapped out our value stream. First, our production personnel created a comprehensive spaghetti diagram of their movements in the production process. (Boy, was that an eye-opener!) My production manager was averaging 20,000 steps a day. While that might be the perfect number of steps for weight loss, it is a terrible waste of motion for productivity in business. In the end, we reduced the non-value-added movement by relocating the entire operation to a more efficient building. The outcome? Reduced overhead costs and a more productive, efficient operation. And, the production manager's steps were reduced to 5,000 per day.

Mapping A Lean Journey

Encourage Daily Improvement: In Paul Akers' book, *2 Second Lean: How to Grow People and Build a Fun Lean Culture*, Akers breaks down the idea of Lean into one simple question "What bugs you?" I asked similar questions of Onex personnel as we began our Lean journey. "What takes up most of your time? What do you find frustrating?" With each response, we worked together to reduce waste and non-value-added steps. The key is to allow the person closest to the problem to suggest the solution, and then implement it quickly. In cases where the process cannot be changed, it is up to you as the leader to communicate (not criticize) why the suggested change is not possible.

Lean Is a Journey, Not an Event: The hardest part of the Lean journey is sustaining the change. You cannot change a culture with an event; therefore, Lean must become embedded into your business culture. At Onex, we made it everyone's job to improve processes, from the CEO to the production floor personnel. We worked not only to improve our processes, but to improve our clients' processes as well. Because manufacturing is the lifeblood of the community, we believe in making things better and doing our part to keep small-town USA alive and thriving.

Grow Your People: Akers also points out that Lean is about growing people. I have always said that my engineering degree taught me how to think, in that it showed me how to solve any problem through a series of steps. Kata is a tool used by Toyota to teach personnel to analyze the current situation, define a target condition, and experiment changing one variable at a time, documenting the expected outcome as well as the actual outcome. The key is to experiment quickly, fail fast, and try again! Not every idea will be successful, but if you don't have failures, you won't learn. Become an organization that recognizes that it is all right to make some mistakes. I agree with the old adage, "You can learn more from your failures than your successes." Just don't make the same mistake twice.

Set High-Level Goals: Instead of micromanaging your employees to meet goals, outline high-level goals and allow them to work together to figure out the best way to attain them. Allow personnel to report their progress and plans for the future at quarterly meetings, and if at any time you feel a plan is not sound or progress made is not in line with your expectations, you can intervene. This new approach will cause everyone to do his or her part in working toward high-level goals as a unit. More work will be completed as cross-functional teams band together in pursuit of a common goal. My advice is to encourage people to think creatively and be agile. It is less stressful for everyone and the results will be better than you can imagine—I promise.

5S – Sort, Set in Order, Shine, Standardize and Sustain: Change is inevitable, but it doesn't have to be traumatic—it's all in your approach. We utilize the 5S philosophy every year to clean out the old and make room for the new. Times change. Don't become complacent. Clients' needs change, and therefore our operations must change too.

Practice Servant Leadership: American manufacturing has been historically autocratic, command-and-control since the Industrial Revolution. Today's global business environment requires manufacturers to become more agile, which means employing a more democratic leadership style where all ideas are expected to be on the table. Onex leaders practice servant leadership, which means we listen to the concerns of our personnel and empower them to make decisions by removing obstacles to help them become more successful. Then, we celebrate our successes as a team!

Today's organizational culture must be people-centric. In this model, team members are engaged and empowered to quickly and collaboratively create value for clients. Leaders mentor and develop their people, rather than acting like dictators and controllers. Leaders should act as visionaries, planners, and coaches. Focus on the strengths your personnel have, and not on repairing their weaknesses.

—— REFLECTION ——

Is your organizational culture people-centric? If not, think about what you can implement, starting today, to be more focused on the human component of human resources.

Chapter Three

Freedom to Fail

Most great people have achieved their greatest success
just one step beyond their greatest failure.
~ Napoleon Hill

"Employee engagement" is a term that resonates in today's society; however, I fear that even though we know it is important in business, many of us do not understand how to really engage our employees. Simply reverting to scheduling an all-hands company meeting and announcing, "From this day forward, we will all be more empowered" is not the answer. Neither is the ever-popular employee survey, as employees are not inclined to answer as honestly as an organization might like for them to, for fear of being identified in an "anonymous survey." Thankfully, there are some other ways to engage your employees that can live up to the results promised in the term "freedom to fail."

Engaged, Empowered Employees

The best way to start is by engaging your employees in frequent conversations, and, most importantly, really listening to what they have to say. Pay attention to both what is important in their personal lives as well as their professional lives, because it will help you see each employee as an individual person. Honest conversation also builds trust and rapport. Begin by asking each employee about the challenges they face in life and on the job, so you are truly able to help them eliminate any hurdles that are hindering their success.

Next, review your policies and management practices. This will allow you to root out the areas in which you can create more freedom. For example, strategically placing cameras throughout the plant does not foster trust. An employee who has their every move watched does not feel like an integral part of the organization, plus it's creepy. It's like Big Brother is watching. Put yourself in their shoes, how would you react to being watched all the time? An employee who is trusted to make the right decisions will remain engaged. No one comes to work each morning with the objective of intentionally making a mistake that will cost the company money; however, sometimes people do make mistakes—it's important to be able to recognize the difference.

So, when we truly want our people to be engaged, we the leaders must take deliberate steps to remove the negatives that cause them to disengage, and instead find ways to empower them.

The philosopher Peter Kostenbaum describes empowerment as "responsible freedom":

Taking personal responsibility for getting others to implement strategy is the leader's key polarity. It's the existential paradox of holding yourself 100 percent responsible for the fate of your organization, on the one hand, and assuming absolutely no responsibility for the choices made by other people, on the other hand ... You cannot choose for others. All you can do is inform them that you cannot choose for them. In most cases, that in itself will be a strong motivator for the people whom you want to cultivate. The leader's role is less to heal or to help than to enlarge the capacity for responsible freedom.

Trust Works Both Ways

Most employees want to know they play a role in the company's success and that their efforts are valued. The underlying fundamental concept that creates fulfillment in an organization is having that sense of two-way trust. You can foster this feeling by allowing your employees to have the freedom to exercise personal choice and to take responsibility for their work and the decisions they make.

You must also make sure your actions and words match. If they don't, and you require your people to be compliant, they are less inclined to feel personal responsibility, and when this happens their full potential is buried. Instead of being an employee devoted to succeeding in their job for both the benefit of themselves and the company, they often exhibit a state of indifference and suppress emotions of concern, excitement, and motivation. They become cynical, believing that those in leadership positions and their peers are motivated by self-interest and are further skeptical of human sincerity or integrity.

Think of the conflicting message you can send by hanging a motivational poster on the wall that says:

You miss 100% of the shots you don't take.
~Wayne Gretzky

When, in reality you are actually highly critical of people who take shots that don't succeed. Instead, your actions overrule Gretzky's inspirational message as you, perhaps unintentionally, project that you don't even want them to try.

Permission to Fail

In the real world, not all ideas will be successful. In

fact, there will be a lot more failures than successes, but we can learn from the failures. When we have the opportunity to experiment and try again, success often follows. It is to your advantage to educate your personnel by providing them with an array of learning opportunities and supporting them when they try a new idea and it fails. This strategy is a win for you both.

○ **Ground Rules for Turning Failures into Positives:**

1. Identify the root cause of the failure when a mistake is made

2. Discuss and implement ways to prevent the mistake from happening again

3. Remember—no yelling or screaming about the error is allowed

4. Do not hide failure, instead bring it into the light so the team can work together to flush it out of the system

5. Create a learning organization where all ideas are welcomed and encouraged

6. Require everyone to take responsibility for

their decisions and hold them accountable

7. Celebrate successes as a team

Failure Comes to Those Who Do Not Try

Now that you know the ground rules, it's time to push yourself and your personnel outside the comfort zone. Failure should be defined as not trying instead of as an outcome of trying but not being successful. If the outcome was not what you expected, continue to try until you reach success.

Sara Blakely, the founder of Spanx, a successful women's shapewear company, credits her success to the discussions she had at her childhood dinner table. Instead of asking, "What did you learn at school today?" her parents asked, "What did you fail at today?" When there was no failure to report, Blakely's father would express disappointment. This attitude toward failure gave Blakely the confidence she relied upon to overcome a series of remarkable obstacles when building her business. She began her business with just $5000 in the bank, had no experience in the hosiery industry, and had never taken a single business course. Today, Blakely is a billionaire!

growth

The road to progress is not smooth or straight. Rather, it's a rutted path with twists and turns, filled with peaks and valleys and fallen trees blocking the way. The relationship between creativity and progress is a messy one, because the journey is filled with obstacles, challenges, and setbacks. When we are determined to succeed, it's good to have the forewarning that there will be problems, mistakes made, and unforeseen issues along the road—having the confidence to experiment with various solutions and failing fast is what eventually leads to success.

Two Different Leadership Styles

Unfortunately, a traditional command-and-control leadership style is autocratic and curbs freedom in the workplace by establishing a rigid hierarchy, burdensome rules, and silos within the organization, as well as oppressing people with unjust authority. This is the toxic environment we need to change if we want to keep talented personnel from looking for another job or, even worse, not performing to their true potential. It won't be easy, but transforming your company is possible—and important to long-term viability.

On the other hand, a leadership style that takes the "coach approach" flattens the organizational chart, allowing personnel to participate in the decision-making process. Procedures under this leadership style are evaluated with a goal of simplifying them to allow for the freedom of individuality, personal judgment, innovation, and creativity.

Personnel share in core values and your mission for the future. This is the moral compass that is needed for staying the course. Your people will learn and improve quickly because they have the freedom to innovate, experiment, and fail within the guidelines of the organizational values and mission. In turn, there will be a constant pursuit of perfection with continuous improvement each day, and work completed by cross-functional teams. Your people will have the opportunity and the freedom to make a positive mark on the world.

The United States Declaration of Independence includes the following line:

We hold these truths to be self-evident, that all men are created equal, that they are endowed by their Creator with certain unalienable Rights, that among these are Life, Liberty [freedom], and the pursuit of Happiness.

These are not simply words from history; these are principles that are still valid today. People thrive, engage, and are more successful when given the responsibility and freedom to realize their full potential.

--- REFLECTION ---

Why, as leaders, do we continue to run our businesses as command-and-control dictatorships that stifle otherwise engaged and empowered employees when a coach approach leadership style is proven to be more effective?

Chapter Four

Servant Leadership

It is better to lead from behind and to put others in front, especially when you celebrate victory when nice things occur. You take the front line when there is danger. Then people will appreciate your leadership.

~ Nelson Mandela

The foundation of servant leadership is a shared mission that inspires others to take the journey along with the leader in order to make things better. Servant leaders take the traditional power leadership model and turn it completely upside down. This new hierarchy puts employees at the top and the leader at the bottom to serve everyone above him or her. Servant leaders build communities by uniting people and empowering each of them to lead along the journey.

Nelson Mandela, former president of South Africa, is an excellent example of a servant leader. We think we have a great divide here in the United States between our political parties, but that divide is nothing compared to the racial divide Mandela faced in South Africa. In his speeches, he referred to himself as the "people's servant." Servanthood was the driving force in Mandela's life, leadership, and legacy, and by practicing it, he was able to change the world.

Making The Shift To Servant Leadership

On one hand, traditional business leaders are managers who function to oversee their employees, ensuring they perform their job functions in return for a salary and benefits. As a positional leader, these managers derive authority simply from their title of boss. On the other hand, servant leaders are able to move beyond the transactional aspects of management, choosing to actively develop and align an employee's sense of purpose with the company mission. This is where the magic happens, and performance goes through the roof!

In this leadership model, a servant leader must possess an unselfish mindset, which, for some managers, requires a major attitude shift. In this situation, the leader serves instead of commands, shows humility instead of brandishing authority, and ensures psychological safety so that the staff can focus on their strengths unlocking potential, creativity, and a sense of purpose. This attitude reprogramming is made easier when the organization's workplace culture helps to foster this leadership style. There are behaviors that leaders must regularly practice that include empathy and compassion (GRACE), as well as determination, persistence, and resilience (GRIT). This means that leaders are judged by their behavior, and not by what they say.

Most importantly, servant leadership is about helping people grow. When people understand their purpose, they feel motivated, energized, and contribute at the highest level. As a leader, you are responsible for helping your people to get from point A to point B. You are their safety net, giving them the courage to try out new ideas, even if it means sometimes they fail. When failure does happen, you are the one that will help your people get back up and try again so that they can learn from what went wrong the first time. The process is much like a parent teaching a child to walk or ride a bike. The journey continues in a positive way, and each time a milestone is reached, it is celebrated, and a new milestone for growth is set. Just think: if all employees were inspired and encouraged to be their best, all organizations would grow and flourish beyond their wildest dreams.

This type of leadership with its serve-first mindset is what I practice, and as such I expect my leadership team not to tell someone how to do a task, but instead to model the way, by jumping in and working alongside their team. This leadership method also eliminates the problem leaders often have when they instruct a member of their team to perform a specific task that ends up having an unexpected result, which is something I know all too well. I used to be the kind of boss who said, "There is the right way, the wrong way, and some random third way to do things." And I never understood why the third way always seemed to be the chosen way—until I learned about and started practicing servant leadership.

Servant leadership also showed me the reason why employees who chose the third alternative always caught me by surprise. When you really think about it, what we say and what another person hears is not always the same thing. Sometimes, in fact, they are distinctly different. This is because everyone's frame of reference differs based on their background, personal and work history, and perspective. This is not a rare occurrence; it also happens in our personal lives, so it's only natural for it to carry over to the workplace.

Getting Everyone On The Same Page

Let's take a moment to run through an example I use with my personnel to illustrate how everyone thinks differently based on their personal history and perspective.

Making a Peanut Butter and Jelly Sandwich

I would like you to take a moment and write down instructions for making a peanut butter and jelly sandwich. As you write, be sure to carefully think through each step. Now, envision reading me those instructions and the myriad of ways I could logically perform the task.

Your instruction: Put the peanut butter on the bread.

My response: I take the jar of peanut butter and place it on top of the bag of bread.

Your instruction: Put the jelly on the bread.

My response: I take jelly and smear it on top of the bag of bread.

Your instruction: Put the two pieces of bread with peanut butter and jelly on them together.

My response: I put the slices of bread together with the jelly and peanut butter facing outwards.

(Yes, it is a mess!)

See where I'm going with this? Although your instructions may have been perfectly clear, my way of executing them was not what you expected. In real life, you would be pretty frustrated with me, but this example quickly goes right to the heart of the issue, as it clearly illustrates that giving someone a set of instructions does not always (if ever) yield the result you expected. This seemingly simple exercise is surprisingly effective, and it's fun to do with your staff. It is also one that resonates long after it is performed. Try it and see for yourself. Before you know it, you'll see that the instructions you and your staff formulate are much clearer and more detailed. Not to mention, you'll have a great time discussing the "proper way" to make a PB&J sandwich. The point is there is no wrong way, but the process might not be what the person who wants the PB&J sandwich had in mind, even though every outcome eventually resulted in an edible sandwich.

Next, consider how you would feel if your boss

told you exactly how to make a PB&J sandwich or gave you their detailed roadmap for the proper process to net the expected outcome. You would feel very frustrated if their process differed greatly from the one you were used to. Instead, think of how you would feel if the boss said, "Please make me a PB&J sandwich and do it any way you see fit." I bet you would be thrilled at the chance to make the best sandwich you could to impress your boss, rather than merely being asked to comply with following someone else's roadmap. What if you grilled the sandwich, making it the best thing since sliced bread? Focus on the outcome and not the process— that's what allows creativity to flow.

Ask Questions, Listen to the Answers

Another very important aspect of servant leadership is to listen closely to the answers to the questions you ask. When I first began my leadership journey, I once asked an employee, "What task takes up most of your time and you find frustrating?" Upon hearing the answer, I responded with, "Let's fix it."

My answer enabled us to work together to quickly eliminate the problem with an eye on continuous improvement, and each time, we gained confidence and built trust in one another.

This emphasis on asking questions works both ways. Employees should also feel comfortable asking the leader questions without worrying about retaliation. Being able to ask questions helps drive the development and growth of employees. Formulating questions is also a sign that an employee is engaged enough to think and question aspects of his or her job or the business which just might lead to a much-needed innovation.

Another crucial aspect of listening is to understand what the other person is saying. Always listen silently while making an active effort to understand the employee's point of view. Do your best not to interrupt and interject your own thoughts while he or she is speaking. (Easier said than done, I know.)

The Leader is a Member of the Team

Maybe the most important aspect of servant

leadership is that the leader does not take credit for a team's success. The leader is humble, kind, and works hard on the behalf of their team. The leader must gain the trust of their followers if he or she expects them to want to be a part of the team, especially if the leader is making dramatic changes. The bottom line is this: the leader is no better than any other team member.

This last thought is very important to consider when it comes to the difference between being a manager and being a leader. Having a management title does not automatically make you a leader. To be a leader means you must interact with your team and value everyone and take the time to listen to his or her thoughts, which will be as diverse as each person's background. Give yourself the opportunity to surround yourself with people who challenge you and voice their opinions. By making sure that everyone is heard and respected, you will evolve and grow as a leader and as an organization in support of true diversity and inclusion.

The most difficult aspect of servant leadership is

that it takes the courage to be vulnerable. First and foremost, it takes courage to sit down and listen to what your employees have to say, because it shows you don't know everything, and you may actually need their help. Also, it's tough to hear the hard truth (because you'd prefer not to), but you need to be able to if you want to make things better. Do this, and employee satisfaction and engagement will increase significantly. What you will find is that by modeling vulnerability, others in the organization will do the same and start serving one another.

—— REFLECTION ——

Remember Nelson Mandela referred to himself as the "people's servant," which shaped his leadership and legacy. Who have you served today? What will your legacy be?

Chapter Five

A Coach Approach

Men are developed the same way that
gold is mined. When gold is mined, several
tons of dirt must be moved to get an ounce
of gold, but one doesn't go into the mine looking
for dirt— one goes in looking for gold.
~ Andrew Carnegie

Every year, near annual review time, the workplace atmosphere becomes tense, and it's like pulling teeth to get managers to complete the required employee reviews. Honestly, for most of us, a performance review feels neither comfortable to perform nor an entirely reliable gauge of an employee's value to the company. This is because the traditional employee review isn't designed to capture all of the employee's "real" contributions. Instead, it commonly links performance to a narrow set of employee goals. These types of reviews may or may not be representative of the employee's contribution as a whole. More importantly, in our fast-paced world, the needs of businesses often change dramatically, leaving us looking in the rearview mirror when we need to be looking forward. This creates a disconnect between meeting annual goals and current reality. For example, a top performer may work hard to contribute to a company's success, but when he or she is evaluated against a 12-month-old goal, this otherwise top performer may be rated poorly, which could have serious implications for compensation and advancement. It's a very real problem for both managers and employees.

I've experienced this disconnect and frustration, too. I remember the year my board of directors gave me a 1 out of 5 for failing to "write a manufacturing plan." I was crushed. I had spent half the year and many hours of overtime moving the manufacturing facility to a new, more cost-efficient operating space. Essentially, I didn't write the plan. I was busy executing it, because I had already identified the problem and the solution! The following year, I requested they assign high-level results-based goals rather than specific task-based goals. In our case, business is so agile that a task set in January might not be relevant by December. The board agreed with me, and together we established goals for business outcomes with scheduled quarterly check-ins to report and discuss progress. The first year we took this approach was one of the best years in our recent history, because it allowed me to adjust and immediately take the actions I thought were best for the business instead of focusing on what was best for my annual review ratings.

Managers, too, are equally frustrated by review guidelines that don't reward their better employees. Some managers will result to taking liberties on behalf of these employees, while others may strictly follow the rules. I tend to give a 3 on a scale of 1 to 5 if an employee is meeting all my expectations, because I always feel there is room for growth. Another manager may give a 5 to an employee even if that person is not going above and beyond. Ultimately, the process can become highly subjective. Because this rating often directly influences employee compensation or advancement, these managerial differences can undermine confidence, negatively impact morale, and create frustration for all.

Dispensing with the Annual Review

This whole process made me think about how much I hated being rated and how much time I spent on my self-evaluation for the annual review process. The board of directors, too, spent a substantial amount of time evaluating my performance. Then, together, we spent even more time talking about our ratings. To what end? At that point, the year was already over, and I couldn't make any changes that would make my score better. So, I did away with our traditional annual review and rating process entirely.

In eliminating the annual review, I joined 10%

of other U.S. companies such as GE, Microsoft, and Adobe. Now, instead of looking in the rearview mirror at what has already happened, we are looking through the windshield to the future. Instead of waiting until the end of the year to review what was over and done—what was really good or really bad in someone's performance—we are having conversations in the moment when they are relevant. We have created a coach approach.

The Value of a Coach Approach

First and foremost, taking the time to coach your personnel means you care about them. Because coaching takes time, you must have a real desire to do it. You also need to have or develop a growth mindset that will allow your personnel the latitude to create space to learn, grow, experiment, and change in psychological safety. Your ultimate goal as a leader is to look for a person's strengths and align those strengths with organizational needs.

Helping People Change: Coaching with Compassion for Lifelong Learning and Growth by Boyatzis, Smith, and Van Oosten, explains that the way you help others change is not by fixing problems but instead by helping them create a positive vision of the future where they draw the energy to make desired changes even through difficult times. A leader encourages and supports his or her employees by instilling confidence and thereby allowing them to achieve more than they ever thought possible. A coach gives feedback honestly and compassionately with the intent of building the employee up, not tearing him or her down.

As you can see, the coach approach is very different from what happens in a traditional performance review based on pointing out strengths, weaknesses, and whether or not goals were achieved. Historically, the annual review focuses on areas of weakness that need to be worked on and improved. The original intent may have been to try to "fix" someone but, honestly, no one wants to exert energy into fixing his or her weaknesses. Focusing on weaknesses makes people feel discouraged and inadequate. It makes much more sense to energize your people by focusing on their strengths. The traditional review process in and of itself causes major stress. We've all been there, our hearts racing, with shallow breathing and sweaty palms. Why would we want to subject a valued employee to this kind of unpleasantness when there is a proven better way?

Back in the first century, the Greek philosopher Epictetus said these wise words, which are still relevant today, especially in business: "We have two ears and one mouth so that we can listen twice as much as we speak."

Keep his advice in mind as you engage in your coaching practice by:

+ Allowing your employees to talk twice as much as you do
+ Asking smart questions that are open-ended instead of those that can be answered with a simple yes or no, putting a quick end to the conversation
+ Focusing the conversation on the positives, like their strengths, and putting less focus on negative items like weaknesses

Telling vs. Mentoring vs. Coaching

Telling is giving direction only and is an integral component of the traditional command-and-control leadership model.

Mentoring is using your knowledge and experience to guide and nurture another through a process.

Coaching is a collaborative effort to facilitate change and growth in another person. To coach means to lead on a journey of discovery, growth, and intentional change. It is not about telling someone what to do, talking about your own experiences, or giving advice.

Build Organizational Bench Strength

All companies must build and develop their next generation of leaders if they want to survive, let alone thrive. This means that as a company grows and its strategies evolve, it must align their people strategy with its business strategy. The best companies identify gaps in their resources and plan to fill them—not reactively as the need arises—but proactively on at least a semi-annual planning cycle.

Allow your employees to grow within the company by using an internal development process and promoting an open dialogue with them about their successes, strengths, needs, and aspirations. Instead of the traditional performance appraisal process, focus instead on more developmentally inspired conversations. You can accomplish this by conducting discovery interviews or discussion guides with your employees on (at the very least) a quarterly basis instead of annually, which will allow for course correction in real time.

I find that asking employees to define their goal for the year with one word works incredibly well. But another approach would be to have them locate a photographic image of what a bright future looks like. Take the time to ask them what they feel is going well and if they have any barriers that would prevent them from reaching their goals. Then, as the leader, you can help eliminate the barriers—this is of primary importance.

Empower People with Coaching

Today's organizations are faced with an engagement crisis that can be fixed only by hyper-focusing on developing and energizing employees. You can get ahead of the curve by recognizing that we all want and need to feel like we are making a difference in the world, and this includes your employees. Many top leaders have recognized this need, and in addition to an executive coaching program, have built internal coaching teams within their organizations. They also encourage peer coaching to create a culture of development with a growth mindset.

Types of Coaching

Executive coaching is generally a company-sponsored perk for top, high-potential employees to work with an external coach. In the 1980s and '90s, executive coaching was used primarily to "fix" a leader who was underperforming. Today, the goal is to help the leader build a powerful vision of and for the future.

Manager-to-employee coaching is where you,

the leader, can empower your people through coaching conversations. These conversations facilitate a work environment where your people will recognize that you actually care about them individually, and not just about their performance. This type of environment nurtures relationships with your personnel, which results in positive emotions, empathy, mutual respect, and caring for one another. It's what builds a great team, but this positive interaction cannot happen without a shift in the leader's style from simply telling an employee to do something, to instead asking him or her to do something. It helps to get down to the personal level. Do not to be afraid to talk about or inquire as to what is going on in someone's personal life. Once you learn more about the interests, likes, and dislikes of the people you rely on to be successful, you will understand what makes them tick. Actually, getting to know your employees will always make you a better leader.

Peer coaching is where two people of equal status work together to sharpen one another's skills. Peers coach each other on ways to meet goals that further the organization. Companies that use peer coaching report higher employee engagement and are better at developing team camaraderie.

Avoid The Peter Principle

All too often companies promote people from jobs in which they excel to ones above that level at which they cannot perform competently. This happens so often that it has a name—The Peter Principle—named after Laurence Johnston Peter. To avoid doing this to a valuable employee, instead of promoting them to a level where they cannot succeed, simply promote them within their current roles. Give them stretch goals, expand responsibilities, or provide more challenging assignments. World-class performance is created when talents are turned into strengths, which further enhances performance. By having frequent developmental conversations, employees will be able to self-identify and express to you where they would like to go and be able to self-direct their learning. This will lead to more accountability, because it gives each employee the opportunity to establish a plan he or she wants to execute against.

The world doesn't function on an annual cycle for much of anything anymore. Advances in technology mean things change rapidly, and we must be more agile in order to keep up. We need to adapt to evolving market conditions much faster than an annual planning cycle allows. Additionally, today's younger workforce is used to getting constant feedback, so they are also changing the way we lead.

This change in leadership begins with developing new communication skills and honing the basic ones. We also need to implement a new coaching process. The coach approach begins with training your managers to understand how they can better connect with their people to find common ground, even when they do not share the same beliefs. Teach them how to ask clear and specific questions and provide feedback appropriately without raising the other person's defenses. Start them off by encouraging them to engage in peer coaching conversations to practice coaching in a safe setting. This will allow them to gain more confidence before coaching employees. By encouraging more frequent conversations between employees you can and will improve company-wide communication as people begin to know and trust each other and share ideas. The very act of becoming friendly will help the workforce unite and build a team spirit to give you a competitive advantage and retain your top talent.

It is worth noting that you need to have a low tolerance for passive, resistant, cynical attitudes or rock-star mentalities. Give people clear feedback and a chance to change. However, if they do not change, they may find themselves doing something else, somewhere else.

——— REFLECTION ———

Think about how you handle performance reviews. It may be a time for a change.

Chapter Six

Mission Critical

In reality, strategy is actually very straightforward.
You pick a general direction and implement like hell.

~ Jack Welch

W hen you think about it, it makes sense
that you need to have a well-defined
plan and follow it in order to succeed
in business, but many businesses make the mistake
of trying to wing it. Navigating a new trail is hard
without a map—in both life and in business. Yes,
strategic planning is often confusing, frustrating,
and time consuming for many managers, but developing a business strategy is really no different than

setting goals in your personal life. To make it easier, think of strategizing as a style of thinking that allows you to define key objectives, implement action plans, and monitor key performance indicators to insure that your most important priority is successfully accomplished. This strategy also functions as the hub or glue that links all the departments, objectives, and employees together, so everyone is working to achieve a singular goal. Most importantly, your strategy also defines what you will not do.

Guiding Lights

Company Mission and Core Values

In order to get to where you want to be, you need to start by defining what you see as the mission for the company—this is the overarching goal that will influence every decision you make. At Onex, it took us a while to conceive and clearly define and edit our mission statement. We started out with the same generic, uninspired, boring mission statements that most companies come up with—the kind we have all heard before. Then, one day after many hours of brainstorming, a light bulb clicked on and we were able to define what was most important for us to strive toward each and every day.

Make Things Better: Empowered Employees, Happy Customers, and Thriving Communities.

While knowing where you are going is important, it is equally important to understand what values you will employ to reach your goal. All businesses need to recognize their core values and then live by them. These days this aspect of business doesn't get the credit it deserves or the recognition of its importance. When I joined Onex, we had lost track of our original core values, which threw the business off course. Having the ability to stick to your core values can mean the difference between success and failure for your strategic plan—that's how important they are. Abiding by your core values helps you rule out courses of action that don't feel right or are not appropriate for the company. They also help you recruit team members who share in the same beliefs.

When assessing your values, grade them objectively so they reflect how you want your organization to be perceived as it goes about delivering its mission. As we found at Onex, our core values are both a testament to how we do business as well as clearly pointing out what we were not doing well when our business was faltering.

Be Inspired. Be Creative. Stay Humble. Work Hard. Be Kind.

The Planning Process

Now that you have defined your company's mission and the values you will embody on the way to achieving success, you can begin the strategic planning process. When you are formulating your strategy, make sure to include as many team members as possible. You want as many opinions as you can gather in order to capitalize on the various unique perspectives and experiences that each member brings to the table. These strategy sessions may be different than the ones you are used to, especially if you've been in business for a while. In times past these sessions were reserved for upper management, but today we know that including people from all levels within the organization is necessary to help gain valuable insight. For instance, including the sales team and customer service representatives will give you a better feel for the voice of the customer. When production personnel are included, you are able to identify bottlenecks and required resources for growth. Defining your strategy brings critical alignment to the organization and unifies your people's efforts, which, in turn, result in increased efficiency. The goal of your strategy session should be to come up with a one-page strategic plan that will function as a guide for the entire organization in setting key objectives and action plans to achieve success. The resulting strategic plan is one where every action plan rolls up to meet a key business objective, which then supports an organization's most important priority. Let's look at this strategic planning process step-by-step.

Priority

To set the stage for the planning process, we must first define our priority. Early on in my career at Onex I found that although we had a lot of good ideas, we were not making the most of them because we were trying to implement too many at one time. It was like herding cats. Today, I understand that there can be only one real priority. In fact, this is exactly when I realized that the word "priority" was never meant to be plural. Making something a "priority" means it is the one thing that is more important than everything else.

The 4 Disciplines of Execution: Achieving Your Wildly Important Goals by Chris McChesney, Sean Covey and Jim Huling is a great resource to use when you're creating your strategic plan and identifying a Wildly Important Goal (WIG) as your priority, which will set the course for your business and your work toward achieving it. A priority defines how you view success so you can set your actions and take the steps needed to reach it. Once the entire team understands what the top priority is, there will be less confusion and frustration in the workplace.

Perform a SWOT Analysis

In order to settle on your one single priority—aka your WIG—you need to think about Strengths, Weaknesses, Opportunities, and Threats. To perform a SWOT analysis, begin by asking your team the following questions:

+ What is your company's competitive advantage?
+ Are there weaknesses in your financial performance?
+ Are all of your departments aligned with the overall business goal?
+ Are there changes to your marketplace, industry, or local economy that could prove beneficial to your business?
+ What areas of inefficiency could be improved?
+ Do you expect your industry to change drastically in the next five years?

After analyzing the answers to these questions you will have a better understanding of the areas of your business that need to be improved. Then, you'll be able to succeed at meeting your Wildly Important Goal or priority.

Key Objectives and Action Plans

Now that the entire team understands the WIG, it is time to define the key objectives that will keep everyone pulling in the same direction to meet that goal. In other words, these objectives are the battles the team must fight in order to win the war. All of the objectives across all of the key business units should be included on the one-page plan for everyone to see. Everyone needs to understand how his or her work helps to meet the WIG, and the strategic plan lays out exactly how that will happen.

The strategic plan breaks down each key objective into a specific plan of action. I cannot stress enough how crucial these action plans are for each unit of the business. Each area of the business must complete its part of the action plan in order to meet its key objective, which supports the WIG.

Let's look at an example in which the key objective of the sales team is to grow sales at a minimum rate of 5% year over year. To accomplish this, the actions the sales personnel take to meet the goal may include:

- Team selling to existing clients to identify other product line opportunities.
- Building vendor relationships to manufacture ancillary equipment for the vendor to sell to the end user.
- Identifying opportunities in new sales territories, markets, or products.

Key Performance Indicators (KPIs)

Getting the strategic plan, key objectives, and action plans right makes it much easier to decide what data you will need to monitor in order to ensure successful completion of your goal. Key Performance Indicators are the quantifiable measurements used to help determine whether a company's strategic, financial, and operational goals are being met.

Be very careful when choosing what data to monitor, and keep in mind that indicators never show the whole picture. Never let these indicators become the targets by which someone is compensated, as it can drive the wrong behavior. For example, think of the behavior are you driving if you set a target for a salesperson to make a specific number of calls every week. Just because the number of sales calls per week is met does not mean that it resulted in successfully winning new business clients. If your goal is revenue growth, maybe the better plan is to allow the salesperson to identify their own action plan to meet their key objective of sales growth. Don't micromanage and get too granular on the indicators, because it will work against you. Instead, set a high-level goal and trust each individual to figure out how to achieve it.

Bob Chapman, the chairman and CEO of Barry-Wehmiller, developed one of the most ingenious KPIs. Chapman determined that personnel who were engaged and happy at work were better spouses. So, to prove his point he gauged the happiness of his employees by monitoring divorce rates company-wide. Genius, if you ask me!

Now that you understand how to create a strategic planning process you can see how valuable it is to carve out time to work *on* the business and not just *in* the business. Trust me, I know most days are filled with operational issues, but it's imperative that you make the time to stop, take a step back, and consider the company as a whole from the outside to determine what the real priority is. This will provide your team with the WIG it needs in order to motivate them every day. Then, they will want to do all the little things that are necessary to achieve the goal.

As with all goals, if conditions change (consider the current worldwide pandemic), you need to be able to pivot, and change course as needed. After a crisis, things are never the same, so we must figure out how to operate in our "new" normal. When stressful conditions arise, do your best not to revert back to old ways of micromanaging—remind yourself that they didn't work then and won't work now!

Instead, remember to keep using the coach approach. This is easier for everyone involved, because it's a team approach to success. Gather the team together and discuss how to best proceed. When your people are a part of the process, they are more than willing to help and hold themselves accountable to the plans they helped devise. Even in the most turbulent times, we must continue to move forward with a plan. The success of our mission depends on how well we structure that plan and execute against it.

—— REFLECTION ——

Consider how you might best develop a strategic plan that aligns everyone within the company working towards a single priority or Wildly Important Goal.

Chapter Seven

Sales and Marketing

People don't buy for logical reasons.
They buy for emotional reasons.
~ Zig Ziglar

I t is hard to believe that in my industry chasing smokestacks was once considered a sales technique. The idea was that salespeople would hop in their cars and drive around looking for industrial parks or manufacturing plant locations. Essentially, if there was steam, or "smoke," there was also heat, and if there was heat, there was a boiler or a furnace that needed our products and services. Upon reaching said smokestack the salesperson would stop at the guard shack and ask for the person in charge of maintenance or procurement. A helpful guard would provide the name and number of such person and the salesperson would drop off a line card and a business card. Today, this sales strategy no longer works as well, since we can easily find target accounts online or research the client contact on LinkedIn, and you can put your efforts into winning them over with your marketing campaign. What hasn't changed, however, is that people still buy with their hearts, not their heads.

Let me explain—people do business with people they like, trust, and find both helpful and reliable when they have problems that need to be solved. Of course, clients also feel that cost is an important factor as well, but a solid relationship trumps even that. Business used to be conducted by entertaining clients at sporting events or over three-martini lunches, but times have changed. Today, people tend to be busier, so new clients usually build relationships online or find you through word of mouth.

Marketing is Everywhere

Marketing is not a new concept. In fact, the idea of marketing actually began during the Industrial Revolution (1760-1840). During this era, thanks to innovation in scientific and technological industries, purchasing goods became easier and more cost effective for consumers than making things for themselves. The mass production that resulted created competition as businesses tried to outdo each other to win over and serve the needs of the growing consumer market. Not only did they have to develop the products consumers wanted, but they also needed to inform them about these new commodities. The fundamental purpose of marketing is to attract consumers to your brand through messaging. Ideally, that messaging is both helpful and educational to your target audience, thereby converting consumers into leads.

In the 1960s marketing management developed into an essential part of business success. Marketers became involved in everything from determining the best methods for communicating information about products and services, to consumers, to strategic planning.

When I became the General Manager of Onex in 2013, we were behind the times in that we had no sales and marketing process. Onex still drove revenue with salesmen calling clients directly. Salesmen had their own accounts/territories. Quotations were produced but not stored in a central location. There was no sales forecasting tool or customer resource management system. Not only did we not have a standardized sales process, but we also had no real marketing experience of any type. We did not perform market research and analysis to understand the needs or interests of our clients nor did we constantly communicate with them outside of sales calls. This meant we had no way to gauge our customers' awareness of our products or services. Our website looked like a PDF file. Our idea of marketing was handing out ball caps, notepads, and coffee mugs with our company name and logo—oh, and let's not forget those expensive tri-fold brochures (that everyone throws away).

In an age of technology, we were certainly behind

the times, which led me to launch a much-needed sales and marketing optimization process. First, I hired a third-party consultant to develop a road map for the journey and an internal marketing coordinator to implement it. This major change was not met without some resistance. At first, there were all sorts comments as to why it wouldn't work, starting with, "Our clients are not on social media." But what I quickly came to realize is they were! Then came "We don't want our competitors to see our work." Well, I questioned, why not? Yes—newsflash—our competitors did have similar products and services, but we absolutely had to make it our job to inform consumers why they should partner with Onex instead of anyone else.

The Miracle of Effective Marketing

And so our journey toward building a sales and marketing process began. Here are a few of the successful marketing strategies we employed:

+ **Internet marketing:** We launched a new

website, www.onexinc.com, that was mobile-friendly. We expanded from only showcasing our products and services to also integrating the stories of the people in our company who make the products and perform the services. This allows us to show our customers just how much pride Onex personnel take in what they do.

+ **Social media marketing:** We also expanded to Facebook, LinkedIn, Twitter, and Instagram. These networks are used to create favorable impressions about what we were doing, and we can do this over a period of time so our target audience could see how we are evolving. Our message is clear: "Follow us and see the cool things we are doing."

+ **Video marketing:** We've created and published all kinds of videos that showcase our products, services, and the processes used to complete our work. These can be found on our YouTube channel in addition to being embedded on other social media platforms.

+ **Blog marketing:** Our blogs are designed to

provide technical and educational information. We use blogs to increase brand awareness, thereby establishing ourselves as a thought leader in the industry. Our blogs are also published as articles on LinkedIn and on our website under the About Us tab.

+ **Customer resource management:** HubSpot is where we store contact information and client communications regarding requests for proposals and quotations. This tool helps us forecast future revenue and stay in touch with clients through targeted email campaigns.

Our goal is to use the tools available in today's sophisticated marketing world, which is built on an advanced blend of both strategy and technology. To be successful, marketing needs to include product development, market research, product distribution, sales strategy, public relations, and customer support—all necessary in any business's selling journey. Your marketing plan must also be adaptable to the various platforms, social media channels, and organizational teams in order to identify and reach your target audience while communicating and building brand loyalty.

Value Proposition

A value proposition is a statement that explains to your potential clients why they should buy from you instead of from your competition. This means you need to take your time and distill the essence of the value proposition so you can clearly and effectively communicate it to target clients through a multitude of marketing strategies. The goal is to know what your target clients are looking for and fulfill that need. If you do not have a product or service a client needs or wants, all the marketing in the world will not matter. Never try to sell clients a product or service they do not want or need, because it might just be the last sale you make to them. It will tell them that you do not have their best interest at heart and they can no longer trust you. I heard a great example of this recently. While interviewing a candidate for a sales position, an employer asked the interviewee to sell him a pen. The interviewee asked, "Do you need a pen?" The employer replied that it did not matter. The interviewee then explained that it absolutely did matter, because it was of prime importance to focus only on clients' needs and wants. This is crucial to a salesperson who wants to make a sale, as it is their job to convince a client that his pen is the best one on the market that can meet their needs. This extends to any business. To be successful, focus on the long game so your client is happy, and not resentful, with their purchase. A satisfied client will spread the word and referrals will follow.

For Onex, providing an engineered solution that makes things better for the client is of prime importance and presenting a total package designed to specifically solve a client's problem is our Value Proposition. Every time we solve a problem for a client, that client gains confidence in our company, and then they think of us as a partner. When they then tell other businesses in the industry how we helped them, the marketing circle is complete. These word-of-mouth referrals are golden because people trust recommendations from friends. This also means the next sale will be easier to close because you both know the focus is on the same thing—solving problems.

The Customer's Voice

When you meet with a client, always ask them to describe their problem in their own words. Listen carefully and then ask questions to build a rapport so you can understand fully and work together to solve the problem. Don't make the mistake of trying to sell them the same product that has been causing the issue. I call this "me too" sales. By using effective communication skills including asking questions and listening to the answers, you can understand the real problem instead of just assuming you already understand your customer's pain point. After all, you can't prescribe an antidote without a proper diagnosis—that is malpractice—and not in anyone's best interest.

In our business, we get to work with many different industries, and this helps us to utilize the best technology from one industry and adapt it in another to creatively solve a problem. We strive to always get better at what we do, but this means taking risks. When trying something new, always assess the risk/reward ratio. Some companies are more open to being on the cutting edge and can take on more risk—others not so much. Know your client. Organizational culture, too, is important to understand when trying to convince a client to make any change. Choose clients who want to continuously improve. Evaluate disruptive technologies in a way that best ensures you are making changes to your product offerings that will continue to solve a client's current problems or meet a need they haven't identified yet.

One client told us they planned on awarding Onex a trophy for coming in on time and on budget. They had never been able to make such an award before. How sad is that? I always try to put myself in the client's place, which means I expect to purchase a quality product, on time, and under budget. But I also know from personal experience how many times I've been disappointed instead of elated with a purchase. Again, by instilling a feeling of trust and actually delivering on it, you create happy clients who tell people about you. But the flip side of this coin is also true; when you don't deliver your client will probably tell even more people!

Every company should work toward making the customer's experience as good as it can be. This starts with an easy-to-navigate sales and order process. Interactions with office personnel must always be friendly and helpful. The service team must meet the expectations of being professional, arriving on time, and working efficiently and safely to make the required repairs. When the project is complete, it doesn't hurt to follow up with a handwritten thank-you letter that also requests feedback or suggestions on how the process could be improved. Respect your client by making them feel special and important. It's good business.

---- REFLECTION ----

Strategize ways to utilize marketing to drive your sales revenue. Keep your focus on your client and not your competitors.

Chapter Eight

Crisis Management

Never let a good crisis go to waste.
~ Winston Churchill

Life is full of unexpected twists and turns. Sometimes you are fortunate enough to get a warning when all the indicators start pointing toward a problem, but more often than not we ignore these warnings and don't take notice until the straits are dire, and we find ourselves in the midst of a smoldering crisis. Then—there are the "black swan" events—once-in-a-century events like a pandemic or a housing market crash that put us face-to-face with a sudden and immediate crisis. Every crisis has one thing in common—there is a beginning, middle, and end. This is important, because it depends on how you, as a leader, navigate every aspect of a crisis that makes all the difference in the world as to whether or not you survive it or succeed in spite of it.

Crisis management is the strategy that businesses use to deal with unexpected events that have the ability to significantly hurt the organization. Crisis management is made up of three elements: First, the threat of harm; second, the element of surprise; and, finally, fast action to mitigate the damage. No matter what type of catastrophe you are faced with, one thing you can be sure of is that things will never return to exactly the same as they were before the crisis. Make no doubt about it—a crisis creates a strategic inflection point, which will require a change to the business strategy.

During my short tenure as a business leader, I have led our company through both a smoldering crisis and a sudden crisis. The smoldering crisis came about as a result of the previous CFO's management style, in which he played only to the short-term economic gain of the shareholders without regard for other stakeholders—the employees, clients, and vendors. This left the company with considerable debt, little cash, and a high operating overhead. Not wanting to relive those years, I worked hard to pay down the company debt, and as a result, we were fortunate that we entered the pandemic with little debt, cash on hand and a breakeven point of half of what it once was. Due to the very nature of a world-wide pandemic, there was nothing to warn us of this "black swan" event or of all that would occur in its wake. However, both the smoldering internal crisis and the sudden external crisis required that I use the same set of skills to navigate each with the same sense of urgency, followed up by my determined spirit and my care of the others involved. I had no choice but to be relentless in order to overcome these obstacles, which ultimately improved the company and its operations. To help give me strength during this time when it seemed I had to make an endless number of really hard decisions quickly to protect the company,

I started wearing a special bracelet a friend had given me. When I looked at it, it helped me tap an inner strength, because it reminded me that I was truly on the road less traveled during this difficult time.

Facing adversity during a crisis comes with the territory, but there is a silver lining to be found within that chaos when you aren't afraid to lead. You cannot freeze when a crisis occurs. You must think about all that can and must be done. You cannot take "no" for an answer. You must find the strength to face your fears head on. Tap into your scrappy side! Above all, never forget that there is always a path to the other side. The road may wind, and there will be mountains to climb, but I assure you that path is there. Believe in the skills you have and use them to help you to navigate your way to the other side.

Managing a Crisis

Once you get through a crisis, you'll see how true my words really are, but to help you think about it in a more logical way (preferably, when you are not in the midst of a crisis), reflect on the following:

Flexibility: When a sudden crisis hits, remember information often changes from minute to minute. In each of my two crises, I started with containment/damage control. During this phase you should do whatever it takes to prevent financial, reputational, or physical harm to your organization. For example, in the midst of the pandemic, schools were canceled, and parents had to figure out childcare options. Then businesses were closed, and everyone had to work remotely, which required technological infrastructure changes. Employers had to provide safe work environments for essential, frontline employees. Household items and food, such as toilet paper, disinfectant wipes, and meat, once taken for granted, became scarce. These things, and more, required us to pivot and remain flexible while thinking outside the box in order to quickly solve each problem as it presented itself, all the while conserving cash and preparing for the worst while praying for the best.

Communication: During a crisis an organization needs to communicate with all of its stakeholders quickly and efficiently. Internal cooperation and collaboration around a common goal are crucial when managing a crisis. As a leader you must isolate and frame the problem while working with your people to apply their collective energy and solve the problems you're facing. It's up to you to fully understand the problem at hand while being able to plan for what may happen in the future. In each crisis, I gathered my management team and together we discussed the immediate issue and decided on a path forward together. My team and I went through the list of tasks to be completed quickly, and together we worked to divide and conquer each one. We also communicated our plans to others within the organization to alleviate fear and to also help them navigate the unknown. Ensuring the entire team understands and is focused on solving the same problem is the key. And it is always necessary to communicate with clients and suppliers about how you are handling the crisis.

Determination: In the midst of a crisis, you do not have the option to give up or to quit. Your prime focus must be on maintaining the business while planning for the recovery. Never lose sight of the fact that you have a team that is counting on you to forge ahead and be relentless in adapting to the changes being forced upon you. During the pandemic, no organization was immune from having to find a new way to do at least some aspects of their business differently. Restaurants, because they were unable to offer dine-in service, employed their staff to make deliveries. Those of us in manufacturing had to ensure our work environments were safe for essential employees and quickly learn to meet client needs by using technology and working remotely. When I remained calm, cool, and collected with a positive can-do attitude, my employees took notice and worked with me in every way they could.

Resilience: Every crisis is a learning experience. With a focus on a positive vision of the future, you will be able to envision how you will rebound, how you will bring everything back online, and what the new "normal" will look like—have faith that your new routines and behaviors will ultimately dictate how the organization looks in the future. This will happen naturally if you successfully navigate the crisis. Do this and you will have not only mitigated the harm to the organization but also, and more importantly, you will have made the company better in the future because of the changes you instituted.

Empathy: Everyone handles a crisis differently. Acknowledging this fact makes you a better leader and will help you learn to understand what your people are thinking and feeling and relate to them accordingly. Past experiences impact today's reactions, and it's your responsibility to care for and help your employees work through today. Once I noted that everyone occupied a different emotional space during the pandemic, I made green, yellow, and red silicon bracelets available to everyone. Green meant "I am alright with handshakes," yellow meant "I am nervous so wear a mask and stay six feet away," and red meant "I am scared please respect my boundaries." This visual aid was an easy way to let everyone "see" each other's comfort zones without any inadvertent awkward moments or hurt feelings.

The Leader Provides Direction

As a leader you cannot get mired solely in the daily minutia of managing the crisis; instead you must elevate yourself and do what your position requires, and that is to look ahead to try and predict what may yet come. It's your job to plan for contingencies and to recognize and accept that trial and error is needed to forge a successful path forward. You cannot become unnerved. Instead, it's up to you to make decisions quickly and change direction when things are not going as planned. Buckle up! The pace is always quicker than expected, and your actions must be decisive and firm. To find a path through a difficult situation, stay as positive as you can so you can think creatively—and that means to take the road less traveled, without fear.

When the crisis has passed (and it will), celebrate the ending, because it signals a new beginning. Those challenges you rose to meet were really opportunities, so treat them as such. Companies that endure the pain the longest will be those that survive and flourish because their ability to reinvent themselves will make them stronger.

Never forget, even though you are the leader, you are not in this alone. You picked a great staff, so be sure to get everyone's ideas on the table. Ask the people closest to the problem for suggestions. Reach out to advisers for outside assistance. No one expects you to know everything—look to all of your resources for advice and help. The key is mutual trust and respect as you navigate the crisis together. Remember, a pearl is created when a piece of grit makes its way into an oyster, and a diamond is created when carbon is exposed to extreme heat and pressure.

When you are successful in managing any crisis, your organization will be stronger. This strength comes when everyone works his or her way through it. There is nothing like a crisis to help your personnel develop skills of determination, persistence, and resilience (GRIT), as well as empathy and compassion (GRACE under pressure). A team is stronger after a shared experience and more able to face the next challenge. With each iteration (yes, there will always be some sort of crisis), this will become easier, because you have built the confidence and knowledge you need to make it to the other side.

—— REFLECTION ——

Think of the last crisis you encountered and how you reacted in the midst of the chaos. Were you mindful to take every challenge that presented itself as an opportunity to learn how to build a stronger company for the future?

Chapter Nine

Leave It Better

A leader's lasting value is measured by succession.

~ John Maxwell

M ost family-owned companies fall in the range of small to mid-sized, which is also the space Onex occupies. In 2018, my husband, Drew, and I acquired Onex from Drew's father, Ric Walters. Since then, we have worked very hard and have enjoyed several years of consistent growth. Today, the company has achieved a level of success and stability that finally allows us the space we need to be able to take a step back and consider our next steps, which include discussing our own personal goals and, ultimately, succession plans. At the age of 40, we may seem too young to some to be considering succession options; however, as leaders we are cognizant that we must always have a clear vision for the future of our company. Long-term business success is not based solely on today's financials, the next quarter's sales, or even the next presidential election—it is about being profitable so the next generation can reap the rewards.

Unfortunately, a lot of small companies do not think far enough ahead, and that means they don't take the necessary steps needed to plan for succession. We all know that it's not as easy as just waking up one day and deciding you want to retire. Succession planning takes time and effort. If it's not done properly, you risk making snap decisions and possibly hiring expensive, risky outsiders instead of taking the time to thoroughly evaluate and promote deserving internal candidates. This is sometimes easier done in the abstract, because the demands of operating a business day-to-day do take priority over determining how, and sometimes when, owners exit the business.

Planning for Succession

The Benefits

A study conducted by Wilmington Trust found that 58 percent of the small business owners they surveyed had no succession plan. I suspect that many owners simply love operating their own businesses and find it hard to think of a time when they will be unable to do it. A major issue in formulating a succession plan is that there is not always a family member or valued employee interested in or qualified to run the business if the owner has to step aside for some reason. This is why having a business succession plan in place ensures the legacy and success of the business after the owner steps down.

I don't mean to cast a dark shadow on succession; the truth is that, with early planning, owners can remain in charge and in the position they prefer for as long as they choose—it's their plan, after all. Planning ahead means the business will be able to go through a stable transition, which will allow the company to continue to thrive, offer the products and services that have made it profitable over the years, and not rattle its clients with any hint of instability. The client is secure in knowing that it will continue to be business as usual, and that feeling can never be underestimated.

Four Options

When you're ready, start by reviewing all of your options. A transition plan requires you to start by talking first with family members who will be affected by your decision. This is because—and there is no getting around it—everyone involved needs to consider his or her long-term personal and financial goals—especially the owner. Here are four options that we considered when thinking of our future succession plan.

Option One: Transfer the Business to a Family Member

Many small business owners envision passing the company they worked so hard to build on to their heirs. Unfortunately, this doesn't always work in the real world. Sometimes the heir doesn't have an interest in running the business or might not have the skills required. Drew and I considered this traditional path, thinking that at least one of two young sons might be interested when the time came. Since we are both fact-driven in our decision making, it was important that we looked at the larger picture and took into consideration the unique generational challenges family—owned businesses often face. Historically, only 30% of second-generation family businesses—like ours—succeed. That statistic is sobering enough, but when you get to the third generation, the survival rate plummets to only 12%. We believe in our boys, but they are still young, and these are daunting odds, and the decisions they make as to how they choose to make their mark on the world involves many factors beyond their, and our, control.

Option Two: Sell the Company to a Key Employee or Business Partner

This option assumes you already have someone internally who is interested in purchasing the business.

Even though this option functions much like the family option, it is a bit more complicated since your successor is not an heir, and that means negotiating a financial arrangement. A successor could obtain a business loan to finance the purchase, or the seller could hold a seller's note, or the sale could be paid for with company distributions.

Option Three: Sell the Company to an Outside Purchaser

While this option may be the best to maximize the value of the company for you and your heirs, it might not be the best choice for all of the stakeholders. When you sell to a third party or private equity firm there is no guarantee that the new owners will leave the company intact with the same personnel or even stay in the same city. In most cases, private equity looks to sell a business again after three to five years. Often, shareholders or investors are focused on short-term gains rather than a long-term strategy. This was not a desirable option for Drew and me, because supporting local manufacturing, prosperity for our employees' families and the community are very important to us.

Option Four: Close and Liquidate the Company

To us, this was the worst option and one we wanted to avoid if at all possible. Consider that every manufacturing job supports nearly five other jobs in the community, and the thought of how devastating this would be to our community if our business closed its doors did not even put this option into consideration for us. Not only would our employees have to find new jobs, our clients would have to find another source for the products and services they need. I understand that sometimes companies have no other choice, but planning ahead lowers the odds of having to go this route, and will give you more choices to consider when the time comes.

The Choice

No matter which option you choose, you will still need to prepare your company for a sale, and this means organizing books and records, completing a business valuation, gathering important documents, streamlining operations, and analyzing weaknesses. A business succession plan is designed to provide the roadmap for executing your chosen option and taking care of the details.

So, you are probably wondering what option we chose. We chose a modified version of Option One. We see our Onex employees as our family members, and we enjoy living within the company culture we have built together. Onex is proud to be known for our experienced, creative, hard-working people who are committed to finding innovative solutions and who treat one another and our clients like the family we are. And, as Peter Drucker and the Ford Motor Company say, "Culture eats strategy for breakfast." This family focus and the culture it has created has made Onex both strong and successful. This unique and powerful engine for success actually changed the playing field for us and helped us to reimagine what the term "family-owned" really meant. Was it possible that the greater Onex employee family could own the company themselves?

Reimagining "Family Owned"

We began by investigating Employee Stock Ownership Plans (ESOP). An ESOP would ensure the company's culture and legacy remained intact while rewarding hard work with a stake in the growth of the company. Owning stock in their own company will lead these new owners to make better suggestions for improving performance, encourage them to be long-term members of the team and work more cooperatively with colleagues, thereby encouraging everyone to perform to the highest standard. We believe this option will allow each employee to feel inspired, safe, and fulfilled each day, because they all will know that their work matters in the greater economy.

We remain invested in making the best possible products to meet our clients' ever-changing needs. We hope to continue to make our clients' operations more efficient by recognizing and creating the products and services they will need even before they do themselves. Our goal is to ensure that

manufacturing is operating competitively and sup-
plying living-wage jobs for proud, loyal employees
for generations to come.

We are also counting on America's underlying
and legendary strength, which is drawn from the
power of many individuals working together for the
greater good. In a 1987 speech, President Ronald
Reagan boldly proclaimed the following about the
benefit of ESOPs:

> *I can't help but believe that in the future we
> will see in the United States and throughout the
> Western world an increasing trend toward the
> next logical step, employee ownership. It is a
> path that befits a free people ... In recent years,
> we have witnessed medium-sized and even some
> large corporations being purchased, in part or in
> whole, by their employees. Weirton Steel in West
> Virginia, Lowe's Companies in North Carolina,
> The Milwaukee Journal, Lincoln Electric Com-
> pany of Cleveland, Ohio, and many others are
> now manned by employees who are also owners.*

When we considered all of the benefits of an ESOP, it made sense to make the transition now and to start reaping the benefits. Being a 100% employee-owned company rewards our hard-working employees, excites our clients, and also keeps the business headquartered in its original home of Erie, Pennsylvania. It also ensures we have the same strong management team and leverages available tax advantages.

Realizing Our Vision

With these changes at Onex, Drew and I are contributing to revitalizing American manufacturing, which was part of my original vision to inspire more people to pursue manufacturing careers. In order to accomplish this goal, it will take more than us, but I believe it starts with people like us and then will spread to the culture of manufacturers who must change from traditional top-down "command-and-control" structure to an empowered and agile workforce. Employees are more committed and productive when they are psychologically protected at work, fairly compensated for their efforts, and see that they are contributing to a cause far bigger than themselves. Today, as an ESOP, our employee-owners and their families, our community, and Onex are strong and healthy enough to remain in the game for many generations to come.

——— REFLECTION ———

If you haven't started thinking about your business succession plan, maybe it's time to think about the future and how you could contribute to changing the world.

Chapter Ten

Amazing Grace

As you grow older, you will discover that
you have two hands, one for helping yourself,
the other for helping others.
~ Maya Angelou

I t has been said that leadership is lonely, and in some cases, I can agree. There are days when you will feel the weight of the responsibility you have to fulfill as a business leader. But, you must never give up, no matter how hard the journey becomes, because others are following you.

GRIT is when you think you have nothing left to give, but you're able to look deep within yourself and summon up the energy required to reach the other side.

GRACE is the light that comes when you least expect it but need it most. It is like a child coming to give you a hug after spending the day driving you crazy, or the dog that comes to lick your face after eating the couch cushion.

Well-run businesses have the ability to make profits for their shareholders and the ability to change the world. As a business leader, the responsibility to make things better for your employees and community lies with you. Being in business is ultimately about helping people. By manufacturing a product or performing a service, a sustainable business improves the lives of the people working in it as well as contributing to society at large. This is what I mean when I say, "Play for all the stakeholders, not only the shareholders."

Wake up each day, operate your businesses with integrity, transparency, and vulnerability, but know full well that you do not have all the answers. Be relentless in solving problems and determined to succeed at the game.

Once you get to the other side, you will be able to look back and see how far you and your team have come. You will realize you are not perfect—and you never will be—but continue the relentless pursuit of perfection, improve each day, and strive to make things better for everyone along your path.

References

1. S. Sinek, *Start with Why: How Great Leaders Inspire Everyone to Take Action* (New York: Portfolio/Penguin, 2009).

2. P. Akers, *2 Second Lean: How to Grow People and Build a Fun Lean Culture at Work & at Home, 3rd. ed. (Ferndale, WA*: FastCap Press, 2014).

3. R. Boyatzis, M. Smith, and E. Van Oosten, *Helping People Change: Coaching with Compassion for Lifelong Learning and Growth.* (Boston: Harvard Business Review Press, 2019).

4. C. McChesney, S. Covey, and J. Huling. *The 4 Disciplines of Execution: Achieving Your*

Wildly Important Goals (New York: Simon & Schuster, 2012).

Acknowledgments

Thank you, Drew, for encouraging me to write a book telling our story. Without your support at home and work, our goal to make things better would not be possible.

Amber, it was with a gentle nudge that you inspired me to start the writing process. And, Aimee, you seem to know when I need to hear "I love you" the most. My sisters, you encourage me to lead my best life.

My father and mother, Bill and Libby, are the best parents a girl could ask for. Thank you for teaching me about hard work, determination, persistence and resilience and explaining to me that life would be full of adversity, and reminding me to never give up.

Drew and his father and mother, Ric and Lyn, were the ones who believed in my ability to lead Onex and gave me the opportunity. Thank you for believing in me when I was not as confident in myself.

It was with the help of my editor, PJ Dempsey, that this book went from thoughts on a page to a carefully crafted story. She coached me on the necessary skills to be an author while paying careful attention to the reader's experience.

Greta Langhenry, my copy editor, was able to work with me quickly to fix the grammatical errors. Gage Cogswell proofread the final manuscript catching any errors that may distract the reader. I am grateful for this wonderful team of ladies who worked together to turn my thoughts into a book.

Susan Malikowski did an amazing job designing the book cover and interior. Susan created designs that captured my personality while being visually pleasing to the reader.

Taylor Smith, my marketing coordinator, supported me by promoting the book as well as helping me when I had writer's block.

To all of the Onex employees, thank you for allowing me to serve as your leader. I am so proud of all the changes you have made to make the company the success it is today.

Finally, to all the advisers who helped me learn and make the necessary changes along this journey: Mike Comerford, Trema Martin-Wilcox, Bob Zaruta, Craig Corsi, Susan Hileman, Lisa Pustelak, Deane Patterson, Donnie Young, John Mizner, Ellen Van Oosten, Dan Zugell and Kayla Adams.

About the Author

Ashleigh Walters and her family relocated to the Rust Belt town of Erie, Pennsylvania, in an attempt to revive her husband's family's 54-year-old business.

When she assumed the role as President, the company had lost sight of its mission and family-centric core values. She used the problem-solving skills she obtained while earning her Bachelor of Science in Chemical Engineering from Auburn University, and was able to change the company culture by using a coach approach leadership style. Today, Onex is a thriving, employee-owned enterprise. Ashleigh regularly shares her story with fellow leaders and encourages them to "make things better" by continuously improving processes.

Lessons to Lead By

The journey to organizational culture change starts with you, the leader. Have the courage to take the road less traveled when you identify that change is necessary. Inspire personnel to solve problems while continuously improving processes. Learn from your failures and become more innovative and creative with each iteration. Know that life is full of adversity, but prepare to forge ahead and celebrate success along the way. Remember, if you lead with determination, resilience and persistence (GRIT), as well as empathy and compassion (GRACE), you can accomplish goals you once thought were unattainable. In all that you do, remember to make things better.

Made in the USA
Middletown, DE
17 September 2022

73322625R00078